D1313871

How Do Animals Use... Their Flippers?

Lynn Stone

Rourke

Publishing LLC

Vero Beach, Florida 32964

www.rourkepublishing.com

PHOTO CREDITS: All Photos © Lynn Stone, except pg. 7 © Dale Walsh ;pg. 15 © Angelika Sternpg; pg. 17 © Oliver Anlauf

Editor: Robert Stengard-Olliges

Cover design by Michelle Moore.

Library of Congress Cataloging-in-Publication Data

Stone, Lynn M.
 How do animals use their flippers? / Lynn Stone.
     p. cm. -- (How do animals use?)
 ISBN 978-1-60044-505-7
 1. Flippers--Juvenile literature. I. Title.
 QL950.75.S76 2008
 591.47'9--dc22
                                        2007016266

Printed in the USA

CG/CG

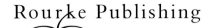

Rourke Publishing

www.rourkepublishing.com – rourke@rourkepublishing.com
Post Office Box 3328, Vero Beach, FL 32964

Many animals have flippers.

Flippers look like paddles.

5

Humpback whales have very large flippers.

7

Porpoises have flippers.

9

Seals have flippers too.

Many animals use flippers to get places.

Sea lions crawl on their flippers.

15

Sea turtles swim with flippers.

17

Manatees swim with flippers, too.

19

Animals use their flippers for many things.

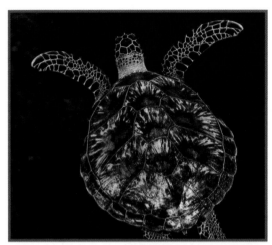

Glossary

humpback whale
(hump bak wayl) – a very
large mammal that lives in
the ocean

manatee (MAN e te) – a
large mammal that lives in
warm, shallow water

porpoise (POR pes) – a
mammal that lives in the
ocean

seal (seel) – a mammal that lives in the ocean and on land

sea lion (see LIE uhn) – a mammal that lives in the ocean and on land

Index

Further Reading

Lock, Deborah. *Feathers, Flippers, and Feet*. DK, 2004.
Perkins, Wendy. *Let's Look at Animal Feet*. Pebble
  Press, 2007.

Websites

www.kidsites.com/sites-edu/animals.htm
animal.discovery.com

About the Author

Lynn M. Stone is the author of more than 400 children's books. He is a talented natural history photographer as well. Lynn, a former teacher, travels worldwide to photograph wildlife in its natural habitat.